WOMEN
WHO MADE
HISTORY

ACTIVISTS AND LEADERS

Written by

JULIA ADAMS

Illustrated by

LOUISE WRIGHT

Gareth Stevens
PUBLISHING

Please visit our website, www.garethstevens.com. For a free color catalog of all our high-quality books, call toll free 1-800-542-2595 or fax 1-877-542-2596.

Cataloging-in-Publication Data

Names: Adams, Julia. | Wright, Louise.
Title: Activists and leaders / Julia Adams, illustrated by Louise Wright.
Description: New York : Gareth Stevens Publishing, 2020.
| Series: Women who made history | Includes glossary and index.
Identifiers: ISBN 9781538243039 (pbk.) | ISBN 9781538243046 (library bound)
Subjects: LCSH: Women social reformers–Juvenile literature.
| Women political activists–Juvenile literature.
Classification: LCC HQ1236.A33 2020 | DDC 920.72 B–dc23

First Edition

Published in 2020 by
Gareth Stevens Publishing
111 East 14th Street, Suite 349
New York, NY 10003

Copyright © Arcturus Holdings Ltd, 2020

Author: Julia Adams
Illustrator: Louise Wright
Designer: Sally Bond
Editor: Susannah Bailey

Printed in the United States of America

CPSIA compliance information: Batch #CS19GS: For further information contact Gareth Stevens, New York, New York at 1-800-542-2595.

CONTENTS

AWESOME WOMEN

The course of history is packed with stories of women overcoming odds, defying expectations, and shattering stereotypes. Yet, all too often, their contribution has been overlooked, underplayed, or just forgotten.

Many cultures have believed (or still believe) that women do not need an education, cannot be trusted with leadership, are physically inferior, and are intellectually weak. Men have been privileged, and this means that they have been the world's default decision-makers and history writers.

Harriet Tubman,
(page 12)

Graça Foster, (page 29)

VOTES FOR WOMEN

Emmeline Pankhurst
(pages 34-35)

Women, however, have been achieving greatness even when everything seemed against them. The leaders and activists in this book are by no means the definitive list of female historymakers, nor are they perfect and without fault, but they are pioneers who stood out, made a difference, and proved without a doubt that they were just as capable as men. Their contributions, both to their field and as an inspiration to others, are worthy of celebration. And that is what this book aims to do.

Leymah Gbowee,
(page 40)

PEACE

NO MORE

ACTIVISTS AND LEADERS

In early cultures, women often had equal status to men— they could be warriors, priestesses, and leaders. But some ancient civilizations, such as Greece and Rome, were founded on different principles. They believed, quite wrongly, that men were natural leaders and that women should stay at home. This harmful point of view persisted for centuries.

Hillary Clinton
(pages 14-15)

Berta Cáceres,
(pages 30-31)

Of course, women are just as capable as men and always have been. This book studies strong and clear-sighted queens, politicians, businesswomen, and activists. They have led countries, companies, communities, and campaigns.

As well as doing their job, many of these women have faced and tackled prejudice. Some worked their way up from poor, disadvantaged backgrounds. They all succeeded against the odds.

These activists and politicians were determined to improve the world they lived in. And they were committed to do whatever it took to make changes.

All these women believed in themselves, worked hard to achieve their goals, and never gave up. Through their efforts and example, they inspired more women to follow their lead. Many of them left the world a safer, fairer place than they found it.

Rigoberta Menchú
(pages 36-37)

MAKING HISTORY

Although history books seem to be packed with powerful male warriors, there are women who belong in those pages, too. Ancient history was recorded only by the very few people able to read and write, so records are scarce. Much of ancient history comes to us in the forms of myths and legends: fantastic stories of incredible deeds – some with more fiction than fact!

BOUDICCA

(c.30–c.60 CE)

In the years 43 to 410 CE, Britain was occupied by the forces of the powerful Roman Empire. It was a time of unrest as the Romans tried to rule over the nation. One of the strongest revolts was led by a woman, Boudicca.

Boudicca was part of the Iceni tribe, who lived in what is now Norfolk, England. She was married to Prasutagus, king of the Iceni. The Romans had allowed the king to govern his own lands. When he died with no male successor, he left his kingdom and wealth to his daughters and to the Roman Emperor. He hoped that the Romans would allow the Iceni to continue to rule themselves.

The Romans had different ideas. They wanted to take over the Iceni lands and treated Boudicca and her daughters brutally. Boudicca would not stand for this! She raised her tribe and many others into rebellion against the Romans.

It was a devastating revolt. Boudicca's army grew to 100,000, and they burned and destroyed the towns of Camulodnum (now Colchester), Verulamium (now St. Albans), and part of Londinium (London). Thousands were killed, including Romans and Britons who supported them.

Finally, the Roman army met Boudicca's rebel forces and defeated them. Boudicca died soon afterwards. Today, a statue of her and her daughters stands in London.

CLEOPATRA

(c.69–30 BCE)

Cleopatra was Egypt's queen when the Roman Empire was at its height. Her deals with Roman leaders Julius Caesar and Mark Antony protected Egypt from invasion. She is one of history's most powerful women. Cleopatra became co-ruler of Egypt on the death of her father Ptolemy XII. She ruled with her younger brother. Later she had to flee from Egypt, and returned with support from Julius Caesar, who helped to restore her to power. Later, her alliance with Mark Anthony continued her power not only in Egypt, but also in the Roman world.

Cleopatra's story has become a myth as it has passed through the ages. In one version she is an immoral woman who caused men to fall at her feet; in another she is a scholar, scientist, philosopher, and chemist.

JiNGU

(c.170–c.269 CE)

There are countless legends about Empress Jingu of Japan. She became Empress through her marriage to Chuai, the 14th sovereign of Japan. She is said to have fought alongside powerful warriors called the samurai. She is also said to have conquered Korea, helped by a pair of divine jewels that allowed her to control the tides. She was also believed to be a shaman who could listen in to the spirit world.

As her reputation has passed through history, it has doubtlessly gathered elements of myth. However, she is talked about in the records of ancient Japan, and in the 1800s, she became the first woman to appear on a Japanese banknote. The records of other countries also refer to Japan as the "Queen Country."

BENAZIR BHUTTO
POLITICIAN
(1953–2007)

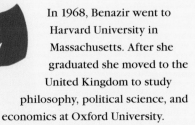

Benazir Bhutto was born in Karachi, Pakistan. Her country was just six years old—it had been formed in 1947 from the Muslim regions of what had been British India.

Benazir's father, Zulfikar Ali Bhutto, was a wealthy politician and landowner. In 1967, he founded the Pakistan People's Party (PPP), and in 1971 he was elected prime minister.

In 1968, Benazir went to Harvard University in Massachusetts. After she graduated she moved to the United Kingdom to study philosophy, political science, and economics at Oxford University.

In 1977, Benazir returned home to work for her father, who had just been reelected. However, that July the head of the army, General Zia, overthrew the Pakistani government and made himself president. He had Zulfikar executed in 1979, while Benazir and her mother were being held in prison nearby.

After her father's death, Benazir led the PPP and worked with other parties to end military rule. She was imprisoned several times. In 1984, she moved to London, UK. From there she campaigned worldwide for Pakistan's return to democracy.

In 1985, Benazir visited Pakistan to bury her younger brother. She was held under house arrest until she flew back to Europe. The following year she returned for good. Hundreds of thousands of people took to the streets to welcome Benazir home—the crowds were so thick that her motorcade took more than nine hours to drive eight miles (12 km).

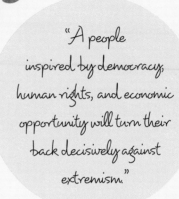

"A people inspired by democracy, human rights, and economic opportunity will turn their back decisively against extremism."

VICTORY GARLAND

In 1988, General Zia called an election. Benazir won and became the first female prime minister of a Muslim country. After just two years in power, she was forced to step down because of accusations of illegal activity. In 1993, Benazir was voted back in. Three years later, she was removed again. Benazir never served a full, five-year term as prime minister, so she struggled to deliver all she had promised. She built new schools, connected thousands of villages to electricity, and gave the press its freedom. But she had hoped to do much more.

In 1999, there was another military takeover in Pakistan. Benazir lived in exile in Dubai, United Arab Emirates, until democratic elections were reintroduced in 2007. Two bombs went off in the crowd that greeted her return, killing 149 people and injuring 402. Benazir was unharmed, but she was killed two months later by a suicide bomber. Mourners scattered rose petals over her coffin as a sign of their love.

HARRIET TUBMAN

Abolitionist, Army Scout, and Suffragist

(c.1820–1913)

"I was the conductor of the Underground Railroad for eight years, and I can say what most conductors can't say—I never ran my train off the track and I never lost a passenger."

Born into slavery in Maryland, Harriet Tubman worked from childhood. Over the years she was a nanny, cook, farmhand, and woodcutter. In 1849, she made the dangerous 90-mile (145 km) journey to Pennsylvania, a free state where slavery was banned. Even here, Harriet was not safe. As a runaway slave she could, by law, be captured and returned to her owner.

In 1850, Harriet went back to Maryland to rescue members of her family. She repeated the journey more than 13 times to lead other African American slaves to freedom. Using a secret route to Canada known as the "Underground Railroad," Harriet rescued more than 70 slaves, putting her own life in great danger.

During the American Civil War (1860–1865), Harriet worked as a scout and spy for the Unionists, who wanted slavery abolished. In June 1863, she led Union Army raids on plantations in South Carolina, freeing more than 750 slaves.

Harriet helped others her whole life. She believed that women should be allowed to vote and spoke at suffragist meetings. She gave so much that she died poor—in a care home for elderly African Americans that she had set up.

HELEN KELLER

ACTIVIST AND AUTHOR

(1880–1968)

Helen Keller was born in Alabama. She was a healthy baby, but an illness at the age of 19 months left her deaf and blind. Because she could not hear, Helen did not learn to speak. She became difficult and angry, frustrated by not being understood.

Helen was six years old when her mother found the tutor who would change her life. Partially blind herself, Anne Sullivan recognized that Helen needed discipline, kindness, and above all, a way to communicate. Anne began by pointing to objects with short, simple names. She used her finger to spell the words into Helen's hand.

"Although the world is full of suffering, it is full also of the overcoming of it."

Helen was a fast learner. Within months she could connect objects with words, read sentences in raised print, and even write with a pen. When she was ten years old, she learned to speak by placing her fingers on her teacher's lips, tongue, and throat and feeling the vibrations.

Helen was the first deaf and blind person to get a college degree. She became an inspirational and world-famous author. Her autobiography *The Story of My Life*, published in 1903, was eventually translated into 50 languages. Helen lectured and campaigned for women's rights, as well as improving conditions for people with disabilities.

HILLARY RODHAM CLINTON
Politician
(b.1947)

Born in Chicago, Hillary Rodham grew up in a household that valued education and hard work. Her parents wanted her to have the same opportunities as her two brothers.

Hillary's interest in politics began while she was still at school. She joined the student council and worked on the school newspaper. When she was getting her degree in political science, Hillary became a supporter of the civil rights movement. She decided to become a lawyer so that she could help to make the system of government more fair.

Hillary studied law at Yale University, Connecticut, and met her future husband

Bill Clinton there. She concentrated on children's rights and family law. After graduating, she eventually moved to Arkansas, where Bill was building a career in the Democratic Party. The

couple married in 1975. Three years later, Bill became governor of the state of Arkansas. Hillary continued her law career and was twice named one of the "100 Most Influential Lawyers in America."

In 1992, Bill was elected president. The Clintons moved into the White House in Washington, D.C. with their daughter, who was nearly 12. Hillary didn't want to be the kind of First Lady

THE WHITE HOUSE

who stayed in the background and didn't have a voice. She set up her own office in the West Wing—the part of the White House where the presidential work is done. Hillary hired her own staff and wrote a new health policy, though unfortunately it was never passed.

In 2000, while still First Lady, Hillary was elected as a senator for New York State. She was reelected at the end of her term of office. Hillary hoped to be the Democrats' presidential candidate in the 2008 election, but when she saw that

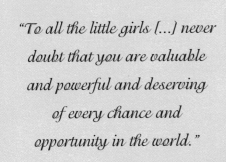

"To all the little girls [...] never doubt that you are valuable and powerful and deserving of every chance and opportunity in the world."

Barack Obama had more support, she pulled out and backed him instead. Hillary was Secretary of State for President Obama from 2009 until 2013. During that time she visited 112 countries and was a powerful voice for women's and children's rights.

In 2015, Hillary ran for president again and became the first female candidate put forward by a major US party. But in November 2016, in a result that came as a shock to many, Hillary lost the election to Donald Trump.

Not to be defeated, Hillary founded Onward Together in 2017. It funds political groups that share Hillary's vision of a more fair and inclusive United States.

VOTE HILLARY!

EUFROSINA CRUZ MENDOZA
Human Rights Activist
(b.1979)

Eufrosina Cruz Mendoza was born in a small Zapotec town in the Mexican province of Oaxaca. The Zapotecs are indigenous people with their own language. Women marry young and raise children, but Eufrosina wanted more. She moved away when she was 12 to work and study accounting. She returned when she was 28.

Eufrosina ran for mayor and won, but Oaxaca's laws did not allow women to hold public office or even vote. Eufrosina fought for these basic rights, and as a result the law changed in 2008. She has since founded an organization to support indigenous women and educate them out of poverty. Its symbol is the beautiful, but undervalued, wild arum lily.

When asked what she hopes Mexico will be for her child:

"a country in which everyone is included, without distinctions, with equality of opportunities."

FADUMO DAYIB
HUMAN RIGHTS ACTIVIST
(b.1972)

Born in Kenya, East Africa, Fadumo Dayib was deported to her parents' native Somalia in 1989. It was a time of civil war. Fadumo's mother sold all she had to fly her three children to Europe. Fadumo arrived in Finland as an asylum seeker in 1990 with no money and little education. Today she is a health care expert who has worked for the United Nations and studied for a PhD.

In 2016, Fadumo returned to Somalia to run for president—the first woman ever to do so. She lost but has vowed to put pressure on the new government. She wants to bring peace to her country, end corruption, crack down on terrorists, and improve the welfare of women and girls.

"I have a calling and purpose in this world. We must stand and speak up against injustices, my family gets that, it's not easy but this is who I am."

DIANE VON FÜRSTENBERG
Fashion Designer and Businesswoman
(b.1946)

> "Be a woman.
> Never forget to be a woman.
>
> I didn't really know what I
> wanted to do, but I knew the
> woman I wanted to become."

Diane Halfin was born in Brussels, Belgium. Her mother was a Holocaust survivor who had been imprisoned at Auschwitz. Diane studied in Spain and Switzerland before moving to Paris and starting her career in the fashion industry. She was married to the German aristocrat Egon von Fürstenberg from 1969 to 1972.

Diane launched her stylish wrap dress in 1974, securing success for her fashion label Diane von Fürstenberg (DVF). Today, DVF clothes sell in more than 70 countries, bring in hundreds of thousands of dollars, and are worn by the rich and famous. In 2010, Diane started the DVF Awards to recognize strong women who transform other women's lives.

SHIRLEY CHISHOLM
POLITICIAN
(1932–2005)

Long before Hillary Clinton or Barack Obama, Shirley Chisholm was breaking down barriers based on sex and race. Born Shirley St. Hill, she was educated in Barbados and New York City. She grew interested in politics while working as a teacher. In 1969, Shirley became the first black woman voted into the US Congress. During her 14 years in the House of Representatives, she worked to improve life for women and children, especially in poor areas. In 1972, she was the first black presidential candidate.

Shirley faced prejudice throughout her life. She survived assassination attempts and lived to be 80. Ten years after her death, she was awarded the Presidential Medal of Freedom.

"Tremendous amounts of talent are lost to our society just because that talent wears a skirt."

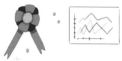

MALALA YOUSAFZAI

EDUCATION ACTIVIST

(b.1997)

Malala Yousafzai was born in Mingora, a city in the Swat Valley in northwestern Pakistan. She was educated in Khushal Public School, which was run by her father Ziauddin.

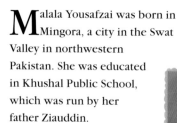

When Malala was 10 years old, a group of religious fundamentalists called the Taliban started taking over parts of Pakistan. They outlawed television and music and did not let women leave their homes.

In 2008, the Taliban banned schools in the Swat Valley from teaching girls. Malala's father and many other school leaders bravely refused to stop, even though the Taliban was executing its opponents and blowing up girls' schools.

When Malala was 11, a BBC journalist contacted her father to ask if he knew a schoolgirl who would write about life under the Taliban. Ziauddin suggested Malala. She started her online diary for the BBC in January 2009. To avoid being targeted by the Taliban, Malala used a pseudonym instead of her real name for the blog.

"We realize the importance of our voices only when they are silenced."

Malala's family was proud, but also worried. Ziauddin was a known campaigner for human rights and female education. Sure enough, he received a death threat in May 2009.

Later that year, after the Pakistani army had driven the Taliban out of Mingora, Malala was interviewed on television. She spoke openly about the dangers that girls still faced when they went to school because of Taliban groups outside the city.

NOBEL PEACE PRIZE

Malala continued to appear on television and speak out even after her identity as the BBC blogger was made public in December 2009.

In 2011, Malala was nominated for the International Children's Peace Prize and won Pakistan's Youth Peace Prize. But she was receiving death threats. On October 9, 2012, a Taliban gunman shot her in the head.

children have the right to an education. She founded the Malala Fund to raise money to help girls who miss out on education. In 2014, she became the youngest person to be awarded the Nobel Peace Prize.

Two other girls were wounded in the attack. Malala survived but was in a coma for nearly two weeks. During this time she had hours of surgery to remove the bullet and reduce swelling in her brain. She was flown to the UK for specialist treatment. People around the world followed her story. When Malala eventually recovered, she stayed in the UK to finish her schooling.

In 2013, on her 16th birthday, Malala addressed the United Nations in New York City. She demanded that all

INDIRA GANDHI
Politician
(1917–1984)

Only child Indira Nehru was born into a political family in Allahabad, northern India. Her father Jawaharlal would become the first prime minister of independent India.

In 1942, Indira married Feroze Gandhi, a journalist and politician. She joined her father's Indian National Congress Party and worked as his assistant. After his death in 1964, she was a government minister. She was elected as India's first female prime minister in 1966 and stayed in power until 1977.

"My father was a statesman; I am a political woman. My father was a saint; I am not."

Indira supported the formation of Bangladesh in 1971, worked hard to fight food shortages, and introduced equal pay for women. But in 1975 she was found guilty of election fraud. Instead of resigning, Indira announced a state of emergency. Her decisions over the next two years were often controversial.

Indira lost the 1977 election but won back power in 1980. In 1984, she ordered her army to attack a militant Sikh group that was based in the Golden Temple in Amritsar. Hundreds

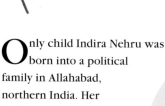

of militants were killed, but so were countless innocent worshippers. There was also damage to the temple, which is one of the most sacred Sikh sites in India. Four months after the massacre, Indira was assassinated by her Sikh bodyguards.

SHERYL SANDBERG

BUSINESSWOMAN

(b.1969)

Sheryl Sandberg is one of today's most successful and influential business leaders.

Born in Washington, D.C., Sheryl studied economics at Harvard University, Massachusetts. There she cofounded a group called Women in Economics and Government. One of her tutors was the economist Larry Summers. She later worked for him at the World Bank from 1991 to 1993 and, after completing her masters degree, as his chief of staff at the Treasury Department.

In 2008, Facebook founder Mark Zuckerberg hired Sheryl as his second-in-command. Facebook was four years old and already huge but it wasn't making money. Sheryl brought in advertising and the company was making a profit within two years.

In 2013, Sheryl published *Lean In: Women, Work, and the Will to Lead* and launched an online forum called Leanin.org. Both offered inspiration and support to women in business. Her next book, *Option B*, was a response to her husband's sudden death in 2015. It gave advice on recovering from life's difficulties.

In 2001, Sheryl moved into the world of tech when she joined Google. Her job was to find a way for the company to make a profit. She achieved this by selling advertising, and was promoted to vice president.

"A truly equal world would be one where women ran half our countries and companies and men ran half our homes."

SHIRIN EBADI
Human Rights Lawyer and Activist
(b.1947)

Born into an Iranian family that strongly believed in equal rights, Shirin Ebadi grew up knowing that she was worth just as much as her brothers. Her father made sure that Shirin received the same education and opportunities as his sons. This attitude was rare in Iran at the time. Girls were expected to be quiet, obedient, and grow up to run the household.

Shirin attended school and university in Tehran, encouraged by her parents to study law. In 1969, she became Iran's first female judge.

She completed her doctorate in law two years later. Shirin was the first woman to be appointed Chief Justice, and was president of the city court of Tehran from 1975 to 1979.

"Human rights is a universal standard. It is a component of every religion and every civilization."

The 1979 revolution in Iran brought a very strict and traditional Islamic group to power. Women were stripped of many of their rights. They were no longer allowed to be judges, so Shirin and her female colleagues were demoted to work as clerks. Shirin refused and took early retirement in 1980. For the next 23 years Shirin wrote books and articles about democracy, Islam, and equality for women.

Shirin was finally allowed to work as a lawyer again in 1993. Most of her clients were women, children, and political prisoners, and she often worked for free. The Iranian government saw that she was a threat. Shirin faced arrests, a five-year suspended jail sentence, and almost lost her law license. It was only thanks to international pressure that Iran backtracked and allowed her to keep it.

In 2001, Shirin and four other lawyers founded the Defenders of Human Rights Center (DHRC), an organization that raises awareness of human rights issues and supports political prisoners and their families. The DHRC

received France's prestigious Human Rights Prize in 2003.

Shirin's tireless work was recognized when she was awarded the Nobel Peace Prize in 2003. She was the first Iranian and the first Muslim woman to receive it.

Shirin supported the One Million Signatures campaign, founded in 2006. Its aim was to collect the signatures of a million Iranians in support of equal rights for women. The government reacted to the pressure by persecuting key members of the campaign and their family members.

In 2009, Shirin publicly announced her distrust of Iran's election results. Not for the first time, her home and offices were raided, some of her possessions were seized, and she received death threats. Shirin went to live in exile in the UK, but she has not abandoned her home country. No matter where she is, Shirin will be pushing for human rights in Iran.

ROSA PARKS
CIVIL RIGHTS ACTIVIST
(1913–2005)

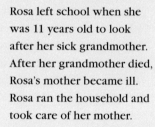

7053

In 1955, a simple act of defiance on a local bus led to the birth of the civil rights movement. When Rosa Parks quietly but courageously refused to give up her seat to a white man, she drew attention to the racism she experienced as a black woman in the United States.

Rosa was born Rosa McCauley in Alabama, one of the US states that had segregation laws in place at that time— laws that kept black and white people separate and treated African Americans as second-class citizens. Under these laws, schools for black children were often not as good as schools for white children and it was acceptable to pay black professionals less than white people who were doing the same jobs. Some states even outlawed interracial marriage.

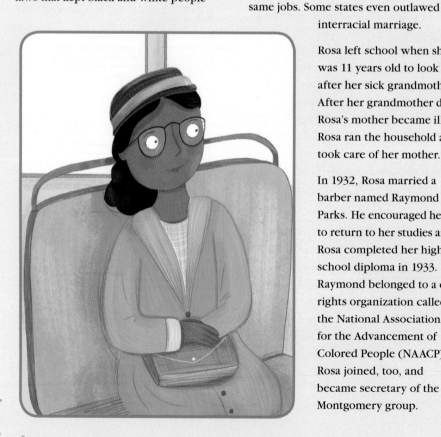

Rosa left school when she was 11 years old to look after her sick grandmother. After her grandmother died, Rosa's mother became ill. Rosa ran the household and took care of her mother.

In 1932, Rosa married a barber named Raymond Parks. He encouraged her to return to her studies and Rosa completed her high school diploma in 1933. Raymond belonged to a civil rights organization called the National Association for the Advancement of Colored People (NAACP). Rosa joined, too, and became secretary of the Montgomery group.

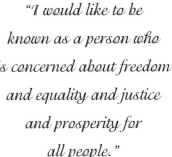

At the beginning of December 1955, Rosa boarded a bus and sat in the area where the seats were for black people as usual. After a few stops, some white passengers got on but all the white seats were

"I would like to be known as a person who is concerned about freedom and equality and justice and prosperity for all people."

taken. The bus driver ordered Rosa and a few others to give up their seats. Rosa refused and was arrested for breaking segregation laws. A few days later, on the day of Rosa's trial, the

NAACP organized a boycott of Montgomery's buses. All of the city's 40,000 black workers took part.

That evening, the city's black community met and founded the Montgomery Improvement Association (MIA), choosing a Baptist minister named Martin Luther King Jr. as its leader. The MIA's Montgomery Bus Boycott lasted

more than a year. It finally ended in December 1956, when a law was passed to end segregation on buses, trains, and trams. It was an enormous victory for the civil rights movement and the first of many nonviolent protests that gradually brought greater equality.

Rosa continued to campaign all her life. She also worked as secretary to the African American politician John Conyers, another champion of civil rights, for more than 20 years. In 1999, Rosa was awarded the Congressional Gold Medal, one of the highest civilian awards in the United States.

WANGARI MAATHAI

ENVIRONMENTAL ACTIVIST

(1940–2011)

If it weren't for Wangari Maathai, her native Kenya would look radically different. The environmental activist, politician, feminist, human rights campaigner, and scientist improved the situation of hundreds of thousands of Kenyans and other Africans, and also the lands they live in.

Born Wangari Muta in a village near Mount Kenya, she grew up with breathtaking scenery. Being so close to nature inspired a lot of her later work. After graduating from high school, Wangari studied abroad and in Kenya, earning degrees in biology and a PhD in veterinary anatomy. She taught at Nairobi University and became a professor in 1977.

PLANTING TOOL

That same year, Wangari started the Green Belt Movement. She had seen how chopping down trees harmed wildlife and rural communities. She began paying women a small amount of money for each tree they planted.

The movement spread throughout Africa. To date, more than fifty million trees have been

> "We cannot tire or give up. We owe it to the present and future generations of all species to rise up and walk!"

planted and wildlife is coming back in many areas. The organization has also trained tens of thousands of women so that they can earn a living without harming the environment.

In 2004, Wangari was awarded the Nobel Peace Prize. It recognized the importance of her Green Belt Movement and also her efforts to make Kenya more democratic.

GRAÇA FOSTER
ENGINEER AND BUSINESSWOMAN
(b.1953)

In Rio de Janeiro, Brazil, the difference between wealth and poverty is stark. While those with money often live in gated communities, the poor inhabit slums called favelas on the outskirts of the city. Housing is makeshift, crime rates are high, and diseases spread fast. Few people escape this poverty, but Graça Foster did just that.

FAVELA HOUSES

Born Maria das Graças, she was raised by her mother in a favela on the edge of Rio. She paid for her school books by collecting trash that could be recycled and selling it. After high school, Graça went to university to study chemical engineering.

In 1978, Graça started working for oil giant Petrobras, South America's largest company. In her spare time she studied, completing three more degrees—two in engineering and one in economics. In 1985, she married British-born Colin Foster and took his surname.

Between 2003 and 2005, Graça was an advisor to Dilma Rousseff, the government minister for mines and energy.

Graça returned to Petrobras, joined the board of directors in 2007, and became CEO in 2012. The first woman to head a big oil and gas company, Graça was included in *Time* magazine's 2012 list of the "100 Most Influential People." Graça left Petrobas in 2015 because of a corruption scandal, but she is still respected for reaching the top in a business that is dominated by men.

"I gave up a lot for my career, but I'm very happy for it. I've done what I've always thought was best for me and my family."

BERTA CÁCERES
Human Rights Activist
(1972–2016)

In 2009, a military takeover brought chaos and uncertainty to the Central American country of Honduras. Gang violence increased, there was widespread corruption, and increasing numbers of Hondurans were in extreme poverty. Life was especially hard for women and indigenous peoples. Many thousands fled across the border.

At the same time, the Honduran government radically changed its policies on managing the land. It earmarked huge areas for "megaprojects," such as mines and hydroelectric dams. The people who lived on the land weren't consulted. They were forced to leave and local wildlife was destroyed.

The state did all it could to silence any protests.

"I am a human rights fighter and I will not give up this fight."

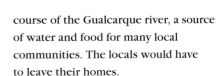

The activist Berta Cáceres (born Berta Isabel Cáceres Flores) was especially outspoken. She risked her life to support people's rights and protect the land.

Berta lived in the city of La Esperanza and grew up with a strong sense of social justice. Her mother Austra was an inspirational role model—a midwife, activist, and mayor who took refugee women into her own home.

Berta belonged to the Lenca, the largest indigenous group in Honduras. In 1993, she cofounded the Council of Popular and Indigenous Organizations of Honduras (COPINH). Its aim was to defend Lenca lands; fight logging, dams, and mining projects; and campaign for more health care and schools in Lenca communities.

In 2010, just after the military coup, Lenca people in western Honduras asked Berta and the COPINH to help them stop the Agua Zarca hydroelectric project. The dam was going to alter the course of the Gualcarque river, a source of water and food for many local communities. The locals would have to leave their homes.

Over the next five years, Berta led the campaign to stop the Agua Zarca Dam. She set up human roadblocks to prevent building materials reaching the site. The army and police fired at the protestors on several occasions and Berta received death threats. In 2015, her story was publicized worldwide when she won the Goldman Environmental Prize, which celebrates the work of grassroots environmental activists.

In March 2016, assassins broke into Berta's home and shot and killed her. Following Berta's murder, the firms backing the dam pulled out and the project was abandoned. It was a great victory but at a terrible price.

The COPINH marked its 25th anniversary in 2018. In memory of Berta, it continues to take action and coordinate the Lencas' struggle to keep their land.

GOLDMAN ENVIRONMENTAL PRIZE 2015

YAA ASANTEWAA
Ashanti Leader
(c.1840–1921)

Today's Ghana has a region in the south called Ashanti. It is named after the Ashanti people who make up most of its population. The Ashanti live in groups called clans, each with its own chief. In 1670, these clans had teamed up to form the Ashanti Kingdom, under the leadership of a single king. It grew rich and powerful selling gold and slaves to the British, Dutch, and Danes who had set up trading posts along the coast (known as the Gold Coast).

By the time Yaa Asantewaa was born, the British had taken over the other Europeans' Gold Coast forts. During the 1870s, they ransacked the Ashanti capital Kumasi, built a fort opposite the king's palace, and demanded huge taxes.

Yaa Asantewaa was Ashanti royalty. Her brother was chief of Edweso from the 1880s until his death in 1894, when the throne passed to Yaa Asantewaa's grandson Kofi Tene.

In 1896, the British demanded that the Ashanti give up their lands and become part of the British Empire. When King Prempeh I refused, he was captured and deported, along with Kofi Tene and some other chiefs. Yaa Asantewaa took over as chief of Edweso.

"I must say this: if you, the men of Ashanti, will not go forward, then we will. We, the women, will. I shall call upon my fellow women. We will fight!"

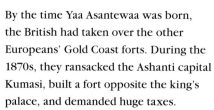

GOLDEN STOOL

Even with their king gone, the Ashanti continued to resist British rule. Frustrated, the British governor of the Gold Coast ordered them to hand over the Golden Stool, the most precious and powerful object in the kingdom. It was a sacred symbol, kept in a secret place known only to the king and his trusted officials.

The Ashanti chiefs met to discuss the humiliating demand. The Golden Stool was the foundation of their society—handing it over would spell the end of Ashanti independence. Yaa Asantewaa was the guardian of the Golden Stool at the time. Seeing the fear all around her, she fired a gun into the air and rallied the chiefs with a rousing speech.

Impressed, the chiefs made Yaa Asantewaa the first female commander in chief of the Ashanti army. She was a smart choice. She ordered each village to build a defensive stockade and won back the capital with siege tactics—preventing supplies reaching the British fort. Her use of drums on the battlefield

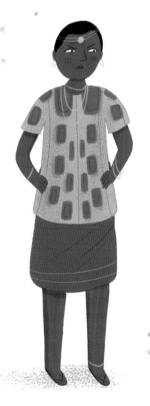

terrified the British forces. At first Yaa Asantewaa's tactics were successful, but in 1901 the British shipped in more troops, overwhelmed the 5,000 Ashanti fighters, and won the War of the Golden Stool. Yaa Asantewaa was sent into exile in the Seychelles, islands off East Africa.

The Gold Coast region was under British rule, but the Ashanti king and chiefs were eventually allowed to return. Yaa Asantewaa's bravery was celebrated in songs and, in 1957, Ghana gained independence once more.

EMMELINE PANKHURST
WOMEN'S RiGHTS ACTiViST
(1858–1928)

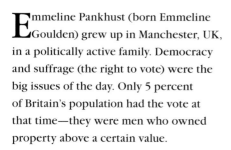

Emmeline Pankhust (born Emmeline Goulden) grew up in Manchester, UK, in a politically active family. Democracy and suffrage (the right to vote) were the big issues of the day. Only 5 percent of Britain's population had the vote at that time—they were men who owned property above a certain value.

In 1897, Emmeline married Richard Pankhurst, a lawyer who believed in women's suffrage. He wrote two acts of parliament to ensure women could keep their earnings and property instead of giving it to their husbands.

In 1889, Emmeline founded the Women's Franchise League. Five years later it won the right of married women to vote in local elections.

BALLOT BOX

In 1903, Emmeline started the Women's Social and Political Union (WSPU), with the aim of securing full, equal voting rights for women. The WSPU's motto was "Deeds not Words," and it adopted fierce and often violent tactics to draw attention to its cause.

WSPU members, who became known as "suffragettes," demonstrated on the streets, smashed windows, and started fires. If they were imprisoned, they went on hunger strike. The authorities feared public outcry if the women died of starvation and resorted to force-feeding, a horrible and dangerous procedure. From 1913, the so-called Cat and Mouse Act allowed prisons to release hunger strikers long enough to regain their health, then rearrest them. Suffragette Emily Davison went on seven hunger strikes and was force-fed 49 times. She died in June 1913 by walking out in front of the king's horse during a race at the Epsom Derby.

Emmeline and her daughters Christabel and Sylvia were behind many of the suffragettes' activities. In 1913, Emmeline went on a lecture tour of the United States to raise funds. She looked frail but was mentally strong. In the previous 18 months she had gone to prison 12 times and spent 30 days behind bars, all on hunger strike.

When World War I (1914–1918) broke out, Emmeline stopped all WSPU activities.

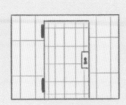

"We are here not because we are lawbreakers; we are here in our efforts to become lawmakers."

The government freed imprisoned suffragettes so they could help with the war effort. Once the war was over, the government granted women over 30 the right to vote, but by then all men over 21 could vote. Emmeline continued her campaign, giving talks across the United States, Canada, and Russia.

In 1927, back in the United Kingdom, Emmeline was chosen to stand for parliament, but she was not in good health. She died in June 1928, just weeks before a law was passed which finally gave women the same voting rights as men.

RIGOBERTA MENCHÚ
HUMAN RIGHTS ACTIVIST
(b.1959)

When she wasn't at school, Rigoberta Menchú spent her childhood helping out in the fields. Her family struggled to survive and often had to travel to the coast to work on coffee plantations.

Rigoberta is one of the Maya, indigenous people of Mexico, Guatemala, and Belize. Her group, the K'iche' people, live in the highlands of Guatemala. Rigoberta's father was an activist and she joined him on visits to nearby communities to teach people their rights. It was dangerous but important work. Guatemala was in the grip of a civil war that had begun in 1960. The army and security forces were constantly threatening people or making them "disappear."

In the 1970s, many Maya, including Rigoberta and her family, started to protest. They wanted to end injustice, have a say in how their country was run, and be recognized as full citizens. People from Mayan communities were extremely poor and had no basic rights.

The authorities responded to the demonstrations and rallies with a sustained and violent offensive. In 1979, soldiers kidnapped, tortured, and killed Rigoberta's mother and brother. Her father died the following year when police set fire to the Spanish embassy in Guatemala City, which was being occupied by K'iche' protestors. Over the next few years more than 200,000 indigenous people lost their lives.

In 1996, the 36-year Guatemalan Civil War finally ended. Rigoberta became a UNESCO Goodwill Ambassador with special responsibility for indigenous peoples.

Rigoberta realized that trials for war crimes such as torture or genocide might be corrupt if they take place in Guatemala. She has urged Spain to demand the handover of criminals and has had some success.

Rigoberta ran for president in 2007 and 2011. Meanwhile, her foundation continues to seek justice for Mayan survivors of the war. It has also replaced the all-colonial history taught in university with a multicultural story that has meaning for all Guatemalans. Rigoberta is president of Salud para Todos (Health for All), which aims to supply indigenous people with low-cost medicines.

Rigoberta went to live in exile in Mexico. She wrote her autobiography *I, Rigoberta*, which was published in 1983. It brought the suffering of the Maya to the rest of the world's attention.

In 1992, Rigoberta was awarded the Nobel Peace Prize for her work defending the rights of indigenous peoples and trying to find a peaceful end to the civil war. She used the prize money to found the Rigoberta Menchú Tum Foundation, which aims to improve indigenous lives through education and political engagement.

"What I treasure most in life is being able to dream. During my most difficult moments and complex situations I have been able to dream of a more beautiful future."

EVA PERÓN
FIRST LADY OF ARGENTINA
(1919–1952)

Eva Perón, born Eva Maria Duarte, became an important political figure in Argentina without ever being elected. She grew up in extreme poverty, but became a successful film and radio actor.

In 1945, Eva married politician Juan Perón. When he became president, "Evita" (as the people called her) unofficially ran two government departments. She increased wages and funded hospitals, orphanages, schools, and care homes. She also helped to pass the law that gave women the right to vote. In 1951, Eva's followers begged her to stand for vice president, but she was ill with cancer. She died at age 33, but remains an icon to this day. Her story is the subject of a popular musical, *Evita* (1976).

"I know that, like every woman of the people, I have more strength than I appear to have."

INDRA NOOYI

Businesswoman

(b.1955)

Indra Nooyi, born Indra Krishnamurthy, studied physics, chemistry, and mathematics at the university in her hometown of Madras (now Chennai) in southern India. In 1978, she moved to the United States to complete a two-year master's degree at Yale in Connecticut.

Indra was a business consultant before joining PepsiCo, the world's second-largest food and drink company. By 2006, she was its first female CEO. Within 10 years Indra had boosted PepsiCo's profits by 160 percent. She also responded to changing lifestyles by introducing healthier products. Indra values her staff. Each year she writes a personal letter to each of her 400 senior executives' parents, thanking them for their child's valuable contribution.

"In everything you do, find teammates who can help execute your vision and empower them to succeed."

LEYMAH GBOWEE

PEACE ACTIVIST

(b.1972)

" You can tell people of the need to struggle, but when the powerless start to see that they really can make a difference, nothing can quench the fire."

Leymah Gbowee was born in Liberia, West Africa. When she was 17 years old, civil war broke out and she fled to Ghana as a refugee. She trained as a social worker and counselor so she could help traumatized child soldiers.

In 2000, Leymah was at the first Women in Peacebuilding Network (WIPNET) meeting. In 2002, she organized Liberian women from all religious backgrounds to hold peaceful protests against the civil war. Eventually their pressure resulted in peace talks and the 14-year war ended. In 2009, Leymah won the Nobel Peace Prize. Today she runs the Gbowee Peace Foundation Africa which educates girls, teenagers, and women in West Africa.

ANGELA MERKEL
Politician
(b.1954)

When Angela Merkel (born Angela Dorothea Kasner) came into the world, Germany was split into two states: West Germany and the German Democratic Republic (GDR). Angela was just a baby when her parents moved from Hamburg, West Germany, to the GDR. She grew up and was educated there.

Just after the Berlin Wall came down in 1989, Angela joined the Christian Democratic Union (CDU). She wanted to shape the new, unified Germany. In 2000, she took over as CDU leader and in 2005 she became the first female German chancellor (head of government). Multiple reelections made Angela the longest-serving head of state in the European Union (EU). Hillary Clinton has described her as "the most important leader in the free world."

"You could certainly say that I've never underestimated myself, there's nothing wrong with being ambitious."

BRANDENBURG GATE,
BERLIN

QUIZ

1. What tribe did Boudicca belong to?

2. With which two Roman rulers did Cleopatra make alliances?

3. Of which country was Benazir Bhutto the first female Prime Minister?

4. How old was Harriet Tubman when she made the dangerous journey from Maryland to Pennsylvania?

5. What is the symbol of the organization founded by Eufrosina Cruz Mendoza?

6. Where was Diane Von Fürstenburg born?

7. What prize was Malala Yousafzai nominated for in 2011?

8. In what year was Shirin Ebadi awarded the Nobel Peace Prize?

9. Where did Rosa Parks quietly sit, in an act that began the civil rights movement?

10. What movement was founded by Wangari Maathai?

11. In which influential list was Graça Foster mentioned in 2012?

12. What prize did Berta Cáceres win in 2015?

13. What precious object of the Ashanti kingdom did Yaa Asantewaa try to protect?

14. What was the motto of Emmeline Pankhurst's organization the WSPU?

15. What was the title of Rigoberta Menchú's autobiography?

16. Of which company was Indra Nooyi the first female CEO?

RESEARCH PROJECT!

Now that you have read about all of these inspiring women, it's time to take a look closer to home. The women in your life have incredible stories to tell, too!

Speak to your mom, aunt, grandmother, caregiver, or teacher to discover their stories and their own experiences. Here are some questions to get you started:

WHO WERE YOUR FEMALE HEROES GROWING UP?

WHAT ACHIEVEMENT ARE YOU MOST PROUD OF?

WHO HAS SUPPORTED YOU THROUGH YOUR LIFE?

HAVE YOU OVERCOME DIFFICULTIES TO ACHIEVE YOUR GOALS?

WHICH WOMEN DO YOU ADMIRE TODAY?

WHAT ARE THE MOST IMPORTANT LESSONS THAT YOU HAVE LEARNED?

WHAT IS THE BEST JOB YOU HAVE HAD?

WHAT ADVICE WOULD YOU GIVE YOUNG WOMEN TODAY?

AS A CHILD, WHAT DID YOU WANT TO BE WHEN YOU GREW UP?

WHAT WAS YOUR EXPERIENCE IN SCHOOL LIKE?

WHERE DID YOU GROW UP?

Listen carefully to the answers that people give, as it is important to record information correctly when people are speaking. If you are going to record what someone tells you, make sure that you ask permission first.

When you have finished asking questions, you can write a report about the person you talked to. You could even include a portrait of them!

Remember that some people might not want to answer one or more of your questions. If that's the case, be respectful and move on to the next question, or simply ask someone else who is willing to share their story. If you want to record their answers, you must ask for permission first.

GLOSSARY

DEPORT
When a person is sent away from a country because they are there illegally or are accused of committing a crime.

EXILE
Being sent away from and forced to live outside your home country.

ABOLISH
To put an end to a system.

ACCOUNTING
The process of keeping financial records.

FUNDAMENTALIST
Someone who follows a religion in its strictest form.

HOLOCAUST
The mass murder of Jews and other minority groups by Nazi Germany in concentration camps.

ASYLUM SEEKER
A person who has left their home country and is looking for protection in another country.

CIVIL RIGHTS MOVEMENT
An activist movement of people who came together in the 1950s and 1960s to end racial inequality. It began in the United States.

CORRUPTION
Dishonest behavior by people in power.

DEMOCRACY
A system of government whereby the people have a say, usually by electing representatives.

HOUSE ARREST
Under conditions where you are kept as a prisoner in your own home.

HUNGER STRIKE
When a person who is in prison refuses to eat.

INDIGENOUS
Originating in, or native to, a particular area.

INFERIOR
Lower in rank, status, or quality.

PHILOSOPHER
Someone who studies big questions, such as the nature of knowledge, reality, and existence.

PREJUDICE
An unfair opinion that is not based on fact.

PSEUDONYM
A false name.

SEGREGATION
Separating people into groups, usually according to their race.

STEREOTYPE
A common idea that can be oversimplified.

SUCCESSOR
A person who is next in line to take power.

SUFFRAGIST
Someone who wants more people (usually more women) to be able to vote.

UNITED NATIONS
An organization set up in 1945 to promote peace, security, and cooperation between countries.

FURTHER INFORMATION

BOOKS

ANTHOLOGY OF AMAZING WOMEN
by Sandra Lawrence and Nathan Collins (20 Watt, 2018)

BOUDICCA (HISTORY VIPS)
by Paul Harrison (Wayland, 2016)

EMMELINE PANKHURST (HISTORY VIPS)
by Kay Barnham (Wayland, 2016)

F IS FOR FEMINISM by Carolyn Suzuki (Ladybird, 2019)

FANTASTICALLY GREAT WOMEN WHO CHANGED THE WORLD
by Kate Pankhurst (Bloomsbury Children's Books, 2016)

GIRLS CAN DO ANYTHING! by Caryl Hart (Scholastic, 2018)

GIRLS WHO CHANGED THE WORLD
by Michelle Roehm McCann (Simon & Schuster, 2018)

HER STORY: 50 WOMEN AND GIRLS WHO SHOOK THE WORLD
by Katherine Halligan (Nosy Crow, 2018)

**I KNOW A WOMAN: THE INSPIRING CONNECTIONS BETWEEN
THE WOMEN WHO HAVE CHANGED OUR WORLD**
by Kate Hodges (Aurum Press, 2018)

**LITTLE PEOPLE, BIG DREAMS: ROSA PARKS / EMMELINE
PANKHURST** by Lisbeth Kaiser (Lincoln Children's Books, 2017)

**MALALA: HOW ONE GIRL STOOD UP FOR EDUCATION
AND CHANGED THE WORLD**
by Malala Yousafzai (Orion Children's Books, 2015)

WEBSITES

The Amazing Women in History website aims to bring
together all the amazing women left out of history books.
amazingwomeninhistory.com/

The Inspirational Women Series website displays a series
on interviews with women leaders from around the world.
inspirationalwomenseries.org/

Have a look at the section on Women Who Made History on the
English Heritage website.
english-heritage.org.uk/learn/histories/women-in-history/

Find out who has won the prestigious Nobel Prize. They are awarded for Physics,
Chemistry, Medicine, Literature, and contributing to world peace.
nobelprize.org/

Find out more about the Kiri Te Kanawa Foundation here:
kiritekanawa.org/

Use these webpages to learn more about UNESCO Goodwill Ambassadors.
The United Nations Educational, Scientific, and Cultural Organization appoint
key people to spread the ideals of the organization. Goodwill Ambassadors help
to raise the profile of the organizations' initiatives.
unesco.org/new/en/goodwill-ambassadors/goodwill-ambassadors/

Explore the Biophilia Education Project here:
biophiliaeducational.org/

Take a look at the website of the Man Booker
Prize to find out how many women have won.
themanbookerprize.com/

Each year, *Time* magazine releases a list of their
100 Most Influential People. Take a look here:
time.com/collection/most-influential-people-2018/

INDEX